MERRY CHRISTMAS
from
Diane Bish

Table of Contents

Exclusively Distributed By

7777 W. BLUEMOUND RD. P.O. BOX 13819 MILWAUKEE, WI 53213

LO, HOW A ROSE E'ER BLOOMING

Sw: Oboe
Ch: Strings
Gt: Gt. 8', Flute Harmonique, Trem.
Ped: 16 ', 8', Ch. to Ped.

from "Geistliche Kirchengesäng"
Arranged by Diane Bish

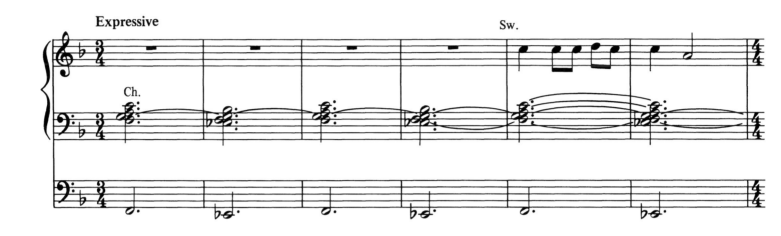

WE THREE KINGS

Sw: Oboe
Ch: Cromhorne
Gt: 8′, 4′, 2′ Princ., Mix, Sw. to Ch.
Ped: 16′, 8′

John H. Hopkins, Jr.
Arranged by Diane Bish

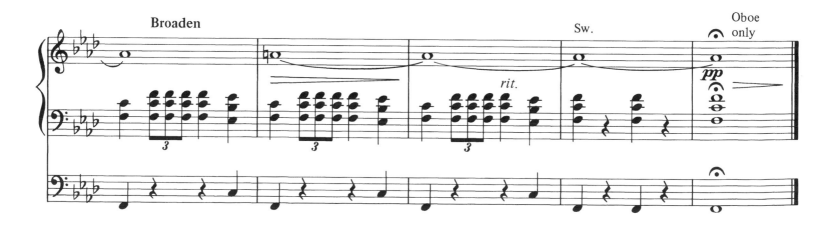

IL EST NÉ
(He is Born)

Sw: Flutes 8′, 2′
Ch: Cromhorne
Gt: Flutes 8′, 2′
Ped: 16′, 8′, Sw. to Pcd.

French Carol
Arranged by Diane Bish

TOCCATA ON
HARK! THE HERALD ANGELS SING

Sw: Full, +Reeds 16´, 8´, 4´
Ch: Fond. Mix, Sw. to Ch. 8´, 4´
Gt: Fond. Mix, Sw., Ch. to Gt. 8´, 4´
Ped: 16´, 8´, 4´, Reeds 16´, 8´, Sw., Ch. to Ped.

Felix Mendelssohn
Arranged by Diane Bish

Allegro-Brilliant

CHRISTMAS FANTASY

Sw: Found. 8′, 4′, 2′
Ch: 8′, 2′ Flutes
Gt: 4′ Flute
Ped: 16′, 8′, Ch. to Ped.

Arranged by Diane Bish

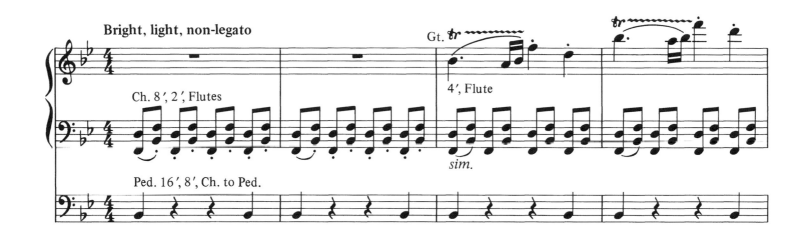

ANGELS FROM THE REALMS OF GLORY: Henry T. Smart/AWAY IN A MANGER: James R. Murray, William J. Kirkpatrick/DECK THE HALLS: Traditional/O COME, ALL YE FAITHFUL: from John F. Wade's "Cantus Diversi"

* If no 32′ Bombarde add 5th in pedal

THE FIRST NOEL

Sw: Oboe
Ch: Flute 8′, 4′
Gt: 8′, Flute Harmonique
Ped: 16′, 8′, Ch. to Ped.

English Melody
Arranged by Diane Bish